50 Persian Appetizer Recipes for Home

By: Kelly Johnson

Table of Contents

- Mirza Ghasemi
- Dolmeh
- Kashk-e Bademjan
- Borani Esfenaj
- Maast-o-Khiar
- Olivieh Salad
- Hummus-e-Bademjan
- Sabzi Khordan
- Nan-o-Panir-o-Sabzi
- Nargesi Esfenaj
- Mast-o-Musir
- Kashk-o-Bademjan
- Zeytoon Parvardeh
- Salad Shirazi
- Halim Bademjan
- Kookoo Sabzi
- Laboo va Goje Farangi
- Anar Mosamma
- Gondi
- Salad-e-Olivieh Miveh
- Havij Polo Ba Mahicheh
- Dough
- Nan-e-Barbari Ba Paneer
- Aash-e Reshteh
- Kuku Sibzamini
- Moraba Sabz
- Ash-e Jow
- Kalam Polo Ba Mahicheh
- Maast-o-Khiar-o-Anar
- Khoresh-e Bamiyeh
- Baghali Polo Ba Mahicheh
- Sambuseh
- Khoresh-e Beh
- Bastani Sonnati
- Khoresht-e Havij Ba Gosht

- Zeytoon Parvardeh Va Panir
- Khoresh-e Albaloo
- Maast-o-Khiar-o-Khiarshoor
- Nan-e-Barbari Ba Paneer-o-Sabzi
- Shirazi Omelette
- Kashk-o-Bademjan-e-Moraba
- Aloo Mosamma
- Dolmeh Barg
- Mirza Ghasemi Stuffed Mushrooms
- Mast-o-Khiar Stuffed Grape Leaves

Mirza Ghasemi

Ingredients:
- Eggplants
- Tomatoes
- Garlic
- Eggs
- Oil (typically vegetable or olive oil)
- Salt and pepper to taste

Preparation:
- Roast or grill the eggplants until the skin is charred and the inside is soft.
- Peel and mash the roasted eggplants.
- Sauté chopped garlic in oil until golden.
- Add diced tomatoes and cook until they release their juices.
- Stir in the mashed eggplants and cook until well combined.
- Crack eggs into the mixture, stir, and cook until the eggs are fully cooked.
- Season with salt and pepper to taste.

Serving:
- Mirza Ghasemi is often served with flatbread or rice.

Variations:
- Some variations may include additional ingredients like turmeric, smoked paprika, or red chili flakes for added flavor.
- Garnishes such as fresh herbs (parsley, cilantro) or a drizzle of olive oil are common.

Mirza Ghasemi is a delicious and comforting dish that showcases the rich flavors of Persian cuisine, especially with its combination of smoky roasted eggplants and garlic.

Dolmeh

Ingredients:
- Grape leaves (fresh or preserved)
- Rice
- Ground meat (usually lamb or beef)
- Onions, finely chopped
- Herbs (parsley, dill, mint), chopped
- Olive oil
- Pine nuts (optional)
- Spices (such as salt, black pepper, and sometimes cinnamon)
- Lemon juice

Preparation:
- If using preserved grape leaves, soak them in water to remove excess salt.
- Prepare the filling by combining rice, ground meat, chopped onions, herbs, olive oil, and spices.
- Place a grape leaf flat on a surface, shiny side down, and add a small portion of the filling at the center.
- Fold the sides of the leaf over the filling and roll it tightly.
- Repeat until all the filling is used.

Cooking:
- Arrange the stuffed grape leaves in a pot, layering them closely.
- Add water, lemon juice, and a drizzle of olive oil to the pot.
- Place a heavy plate on top to prevent the dolmeh from unwrapping during cooking.
- Simmer until the rice is fully cooked and the grape leaves are tender.

Serving:
- Dolmeh is often served with yogurt on the side.
- It can be enjoyed warm or at room temperature.

Variations:
- Vegetarian versions may replace meat with additional rice or incorporate ingredients like raisins and currants.
- Dolmeh can also be made with other vegetables such as bell peppers or zucchinis.

"Dolmeh" showcases the art of Persian stuffed dishes, offering a delightful combination of flavors and textures.

Kashk-e Bademjan

Ingredients:
- Eggplants
- Onion, finely chopped
- Garlic, minced
- Kashk (liquid whey, often fermented, and available in Middle Eastern or Persian grocery stores)
- Olive oil
- Mint, dried or fresh (for garnish)
- Salt and pepper to taste

Preparation:
- Roast or grill the eggplants until the skin is charred, and the flesh is soft. Allow them to cool, then peel and mash the eggplants.

Cooking:
- In a pan, sauté finely chopped onions and minced garlic in olive oil until they are golden.
- Add the mashed eggplants to the pan and continue to cook and stir.
- Pour in kashk, stirring to combine. Allow the mixture to simmer until it thickens.
- Season with salt and pepper to taste.

Serving:
- Transfer the Kashk-e Bademjan to a serving dish.
- Drizzle olive oil on top and garnish with dried or fresh mint.

Accompaniments:
- Kashk-e Bademjan is commonly served with flatbread or as a side dish with rice.

Variations:
- Some recipes may include additional ingredients like ground walnuts for extra texture and flavor.
- Adjust the thickness of the dish by adding more or less kashk according to personal preference.

Kashk-e Bademjan is appreciated for its smooth and velvety texture, combined with the distinctive taste of kashk and the smokiness of roasted eggplants. It is a beloved dish in Persian cuisine and is often enjoyed as part of a mezze spread or as an appetizer.

Borani Esfenaj

Ingredients:
- Fresh spinach, washed and chopped
- Yogurt (Greek or strained yogurt is commonly used)
- Garlic, minced
- Olive oil
- Ground turmeric
- Salt and pepper to taste
- Optional: Crushed red pepper flakes for heat
- Optional: Dried mint or fresh mint for garnish

Cooking:
- Sauté minced garlic in olive oil until fragrant but not browned.
- Add chopped spinach to the pan and cook until wilted.
- In a separate bowl, mix yogurt with a bit of salt, ground turmeric, and optional crushed red pepper flakes.
- Combine the cooked spinach with the yogurt mixture, stirring well to blend the flavors.
- Adjust salt and pepper to taste.

Serving:
- Transfer the Borani Esfenaj to a serving dish.
- Drizzle with olive oil and garnish with dried or fresh mint if desired.

Accompaniments:
- Borani Esfenaj is typically served with flatbread (such as lavash or naan) or alongside rice.

Variations:
- Some variations may include chopped onions or shallots sautéed along with garlic for added flavor.
- Crushed walnuts or ground coriander can be incorporated for additional texture and depth.

Borani Esfenaj showcases the use of yogurt in Persian cuisine, providing a creamy and tangy contrast to the earthy flavors of spinach. It's a versatile dish that can be enjoyed as a side or appetizer in Iranian meals.

Maast-o-Khiar

Ingredients:
- Greek yogurt or strained yogurt
- Cucumbers, finely chopped or grated
- Fresh mint, chopped
- Dill, chopped
- Garlic, minced
- Salt and pepper to taste
- Optional: Dried mint for garnish
- Optional: Raisins or chopped walnuts for added texture (some variations include these)

Preparation:
- If using regular yogurt, you may want to strain it through cheesecloth for a thicker consistency.
- Peel and finely chop or grate the cucumbers. You can squeeze out excess water if using grated cucumbers.

Mixing:
- In a bowl, combine the yogurt, chopped cucumbers, minced garlic, chopped mint, and chopped dill.
- Stir well to ensure all ingredients are evenly distributed.

Seasoning:
- Season with salt and pepper to taste. Adjust the seasoning based on your preference.

Chilling:
- Refrigerate the Maast-o-Khiar for at least an hour before serving to allow the flavors to meld.

Serving:
- Before serving, you can garnish with dried mint and, if you like, add a sprinkle of raisins or chopped walnuts for additional flavor and texture.

Accompaniments:
- Maast-o-Khiar is commonly served as a side dish with Iranian main courses, especially grilled meats and rice dishes.

Maast-o-Khiar is known for its cool and refreshing taste, making it a perfect complement to spicier or more flavorful dishes. It's a staple in Persian cuisine and a popular choice during hot weather.

Olivieh Salad

Ingredients:

- Potatoes, boiled, peeled, and diced
- Cooked chicken breast, finely chopped
- Hard-boiled eggs, chopped
- Green peas, cooked
- Pickles, finely chopped
- Carrots, boiled and diced
- Mayonnaise
- Dijon mustard (optional)
- Salt and pepper to taste
- Lemon juice (optional)

Instructions:

Prepare Ingredients:
- Boil potatoes and carrots until tender. Allow them to cool before peeling and dicing.
- Boil the chicken breast until fully cooked, then finely chop it.
- Hard-boil eggs, cool them, and chop them.
- Cook green peas according to package instructions.

Mixing:
- In a large mixing bowl, combine the diced potatoes, chopped chicken, hard-boiled eggs, chopped pickles, diced carrots, and cooked peas.

Dressing:
- Add mayonnaise to the mixture, adjusting the amount based on personal preference. Some recipes also include Dijon mustard for added flavor.
- Season with salt and pepper to taste.
- If desired, add a squeeze of lemon juice for freshness.

Mix Well:
- Gently mix all the ingredients until well combined and evenly coated with the dressing.

Chilling:
- Refrigerate the Olivieh Salad for at least a few hours before serving to allow the flavors to meld.

Serving:
- Garnish with additional chopped herbs, if desired, before serving.

Olivieh Salad is a versatile dish and can be served as a side dish or as a filling for sandwiches. It's a beloved part of Persian cuisine, often enjoyed during festive occasions and family gatherings.

Hummus-e-Bademjan

Ingredients:

- Eggplants (aubergines), roasted or grilled
- Tahini (sesame paste)
- Garlic cloves, minced
- Lemon juice, freshly squeezed
- Olive oil
- Salt and pepper to taste
- Optional: Ground cumin or smoked paprika for additional flavor
- Optional: Chopped fresh parsley or mint for garnish

Instructions:

Roasting Eggplants:
- Preheat the oven or grill. Roast the whole eggplants until the skin is charred, and the flesh becomes soft. Alternatively, you can grill them for a smoky flavor.
- Allow the roasted eggplants to cool, then peel off the charred skin.

Blending:
- In a food processor or blender, combine the roasted eggplant, tahini, minced garlic, and lemon juice.
- Blend until the mixture is smooth and creamy.

Seasoning:
- Add salt, pepper, and any optional spices (such as ground cumin or smoked paprika) to taste.
- Adjust the consistency by adding olive oil gradually while blending.

Chilling:
- Transfer the Hummus-e-Bademjan to a serving dish and refrigerate for at least an hour to allow the flavors to meld.

Serving:
- Drizzle olive oil on top and garnish with chopped fresh parsley or mint before serving.

Accompaniments:
- Serve Hummus-e-Bademjan with flatbread (like lavash or pita), crackers, or as part of a mezze platter.

Hummus-e-Bademjan is a delightful dip that showcases the rich and smoky flavor of roasted eggplant, complemented by the nuttiness of tahini and the brightness of lemon. It's a popular choice in Persian cuisine and adds a unique twist to the traditional hummus.

Sabzi Khordan

Ingredients:

- Fresh herbs (a combination of parsley, cilantro, mint, tarragon, and dill)
- Radishes, washed and trimmed
- Spring onions (green onions), washed
- Feta cheese (optional)
- Walnuts (optional)
- Lavash or flatbread for serving

Instructions:

Prepare Fresh Herbs:
- Wash and finely chop a variety of fresh herbs. Parsley, cilantro, mint, tarragon, and dill are commonly used.

Radishes and Spring Onions:
- Wash and trim radishes, leaving them whole or slicing them thinly.
- Wash spring onions and cut them into manageable lengths.

Assembling:
- Arrange the fresh herbs, radishes, and spring onions on a platter.
- Optionally, crumble feta cheese over the herbs and add walnuts for extra flavor and texture.

Serving:
- Serve Sabzi Khordan as a side dish with lavash or flatbread.

Eating Etiquette:
- In Persian dining tradition, individuals can take a piece of lavash, place a variety of fresh herbs, radishes, and spring onions on it, and roll it into a wrap.

Accompaniments:
- Sabzi Khordan is often served alongside main courses such as kebabs, rice dishes, and stews.

Variations:
- Some variations may include additional herbs like chives or basil.
- Some versions incorporate other fresh vegetables like cucumbers or cherry tomatoes.

Sabzi Khordan is celebrated for its freshness and the vibrant array of flavors it adds to a meal. It not only enhances the overall dining experience but also reflects the importance of herbs in Persian culinary traditions.

Nan-o-Panir-o-Sabzi

Ingredients:

- Flatbread (such as Lavash or Barbari)
- Feta cheese or a similar type of white cheese
- Fresh herbs (a combination of mint, parsley, cilantro, tarragon, and green onions)
- Radishes, washed and trimmed
- Optional: Butter or clotted cream (sarshir) for spreading

Instructions:

Prepare Fresh Herbs:
- Wash and finely chop a variety of fresh herbs, including mint, parsley, cilantro, tarragon, and green onions.

Cheese:
- Cut the feta cheese or similar white cheese into small cubes or crumble it.

Radishes:
- Wash and trim radishes, leaving them whole or slicing them thinly.

Flatbread:
- Warm the flatbread briefly, either in an oven or on a griddle, to make it more pliable.

Assembling:
- Lay out the flatbread on a serving plate.
- Place the cheese, fresh herbs, and radishes on the flatbread, creating an arrangement that covers the surface.

Spreading:
- Optionally, spread a thin layer of butter or clotted cream on the flatbread before adding the toppings.

Serving:
- Serve Nan-o-Panir-o-Sabzi as an open-faced sandwich or wrap the flatbread around the fillings.

Accompaniments:
- Nan-o-Panir-o-Sabzi is often accompanied by tea, black tea being a popular choice in Iran.

This simple and wholesome combination allows you to enjoy the flavors of fresh herbs, the creaminess of cheese, and the texture of flatbread. Nan-o-Panir-o-Sabzi is a versatile dish that can be enjoyed for breakfast, as a snack, or as part of a larger meal.

Nargesi Esfenaj

Ingredients:

- Fresh spinach, washed and chopped
- Eggs
- Onion, finely chopped
- Garlic, minced
- Olive oil
- Salt and pepper to taste
- Optional: Turmeric for color and flavor
- Optional: Feta cheese, crumbled (for garnish)

Instructions:

Sautéing Aromatics:
- In a pan, heat olive oil over medium heat.
- Sauté finely chopped onions until translucent.
- Add minced garlic and continue to sauté until aromatic.

Cooking Spinach:
- Add the chopped spinach to the pan.
- If using turmeric, sprinkle a small amount for color and flavor.
- Cook the spinach until it wilts and most of the moisture evaporates.

Creating Wells for Eggs:
- Make small wells or indentations in the spinach mixture with the back of a spoon.
- Crack an egg into each well.

Seasoning:
- Season the eggs with salt and pepper.

Covering and Cooking:
- Cover the pan and let the eggs cook to your desired doneness. This might take a few minutes, depending on whether you prefer runny or fully cooked eggs.

Garnishing:
- Optional: Crumble feta cheese over the top for added richness and flavor.

Serving:
- Once the eggs are cooked to your liking, serve Nargesi Esfenaj hot.

Accompaniments:

- Nargesi Esfenaj can be enjoyed with flatbread, pita, or crusty bread.

Nargesi Esfenaj is a delicious and comforting dish that showcases the natural flavors of spinach and eggs. It's a popular choice for a wholesome and satisfying meal in Persian cuisine.

Mast-o-Musir

Ingredients:

- Greek yogurt or strained yogurt
- Shallots (musir), finely chopped
- Salt, to taste
- Dried mint, crushed
- Optional: Ground black pepper
- Optional: Crushed walnuts for garnish

Instructions:

Prepare Shallots:
- Peel and finely chop the shallots (musir). Ensure that they are finely minced for a smooth texture in the dip.

Mixing:
- In a bowl, combine the Greek yogurt with the chopped shallots.

Seasoning:
- Add salt to taste. Remember that yogurt dips can tolerate a good amount of salt, so adjust according to your preference.
- Sprinkle crushed dried mint over the yogurt and shallot mixture. Optionally, add ground black pepper for additional flavor.

Mix Well:
- Stir the ingredients thoroughly to ensure an even distribution of shallots, mint, and seasoning throughout the yogurt.

Chilling:
- Refrigerate the Mast-o-Musir for at least an hour to allow the flavors to meld.

Serving:
- Before serving, garnish with crushed walnuts if desired.

Accompaniments:
- Mast-o-Musir is commonly served as a side dish or condiment with various Persian dishes, grilled meats, or as part of a mezze spread.
- Enjoy it with flatbread, pita, or as a refreshing side to rice-based dishes.

Mast-o-Musir is appreciated for its creamy texture, the sharpness of shallots, and the aromatic touch of dried mint. It adds a delightful contrast and depth of flavor to meals in Persian cuisine.

Kashk-o-Bademjan

Ingredients:

- Eggplants (aubergines)
- Kashk (liquid whey, often fermented, available in Middle Eastern or Persian grocery stores)
- Onion, finely chopped
- Garlic, minced
- Mint, dried or fresh
- Olive oil
- Salt and pepper to taste

Instructions:

Roast or Grill Eggplants:
- Roast or grill the eggplants until the skin is charred and the flesh is soft. Allow them to cool, then peel and mash the eggplants.

Sauté Aromatics:
- In a pan, sauté finely chopped onions in olive oil until golden.
- Add minced garlic to the pan and continue sautéing until aromatic.

Combine with Eggplants:
- Add the mashed roasted eggplants to the pan and stir well, allowing the flavors to meld.

Add Kashk:
- Pour in the kashk, stirring continuously to create a smooth and creamy mixture. Adjust the quantity of kashk based on your preference.

Seasoning:
- Season with salt and pepper to taste. The kashk itself is often salty, so be mindful of the overall saltiness.

Simmer:
- Allow the mixture to simmer on low heat, ensuring it thickens to the desired consistency.

Garnish:
- Garnish with dried or fresh mint, and drizzle olive oil on top before serving.

Serving:
- Serve Kashk-o-Bademjan warm with flatbread, such as lavash or pita.

Kashk-o-Bademjan is appreciated for its creamy texture, smoky flavor from the roasted eggplants, and the unique tanginess contributed by kashk. It's a flavorful and distinctive dish in Persian cuisine.

Zeytoon Parvardeh

Ingredients:

- Green or black olives, pitted
- Walnuts, finely chopped
- Garlic cloves, minced
- Fresh herbs (such as mint and parsley), finely chopped
- Pomegranate molasses
- Olive oil
- Ground cumin (optional)
- Crushed red pepper flakes (optional, for heat)
- Salt to taste

Instructions:

Prepare Olives:
- If your olives are not pitted, make sure to pit them. You can use green or black olives based on your preference.

Mixing:
- In a bowl, combine the pitted olives, finely chopped walnuts, minced garlic, and chopped fresh herbs.

Add Flavorings:
- Add a generous drizzle of olive oil and pomegranate molasses to the mixture.
- Optionally, sprinkle ground cumin for added depth of flavor.
- Add a pinch of crushed red pepper flakes if you want a bit of heat.

Seasoning:
- Season the Zeytoon Parvardeh with salt to taste. Remember that olives can be naturally salty, so adjust accordingly.

Marinate:
- Mix all the ingredients thoroughly to ensure the olives are well coated with the marinade.
- Allow the Zeytoon Parvardeh to marinate in the refrigerator for at least a couple of hours or overnight. This allows the flavors to meld.

Serving:
- Before serving, bring the Zeytoon Parvardeh to room temperature.
- Serve it as a side dish, appetizer, or as part of a mezze spread.

Zeytoon Parvardeh is appreciated for its vibrant flavors, combining the brininess of olives with the richness of walnuts and the sweet-tart notes from pomegranate molasses. It's a delightful addition to Persian cuisine and can be enjoyed in various ways.

Salad Shirazi

Ingredients:

- Cucumbers, diced
- Tomatoes, diced
- Red onion, finely chopped
- Fresh mint, chopped
- Fresh parsley, chopped
- Lemon juice
- Olive oil
- Salt and pepper to taste

Instructions:

Prepare Vegetables:
- Wash and dice the cucumbers and tomatoes. Finely chop the red onion.

Chop Fresh Herbs:
- Chop fresh mint and parsley. These herbs add a burst of flavor and freshness to the salad.

Combine Ingredients:
- In a large mixing bowl, combine the diced cucumbers, tomatoes, chopped red onion, fresh mint, and fresh parsley.

Dress the Salad:
- Drizzle olive oil over the salad.
- Squeeze fresh lemon juice onto the vegetables. Adjust the amount based on your preference for acidity.

Seasoning:
- Sprinkle salt and pepper to taste. Toss the salad to ensure even distribution of the dressing and seasonings.

Chill:
- Allow the Salad Shirazi to chill in the refrigerator for at least 30 minutes before serving. This enhances the flavors.

Serving:
- Serve Salad Shirazi as a side dish, part of a mezze spread, or as a refreshing accompaniment to grilled meats.

Optional Additions:

- Some variations of Salad Shirazi may include a touch of ground sumac for added tanginess.
- You can add a small amount of crushed garlic for extra flavor.

Note:

- Salad Shirazi is often served during hot weather due to its cooling and hydrating qualities.

This light and vibrant Salad Shirazi is a popular and versatile dish in Persian cuisine, celebrated for its simplicity and the use of fresh, seasonal ingredients.

Halim Bademjan

Halim Recipe:

Ingredients:

- 1 cup whole wheat grains
- 1 cup shredded or finely chopped cooked chicken or beef
- 1 large onion, finely chopped
- 1 teaspoon turmeric
- Salt, to taste
- Water
- Garnishes: Cinnamon, butter, and fried onions

Instructions:

Rinse the wheat grains under cold water.
In a large pot, combine the wheat grains with about 4 cups of water and bring to a boil.
Reduce heat and simmer, stirring occasionally, until the wheat becomes soft and starts to blend with water (this may take several hours).
In a separate pan, sauté chopped onions in a bit of oil until golden brown.
Add the cooked meat, turmeric, and salt to the onions. Cook until well combined.
Add the meat mixture to the pot with the wheat and continue simmering, stirring occasionally, until the mixture thickens to a porridge-like consistency.
Adjust salt and spices to taste.
Serve Halim hot, garnished with a sprinkle of cinnamon, a dollop of butter, and fried onions.

Kashk-e Bademjan Recipe:

Ingredients:

- 2 large eggplants
- 1 cup kashk (liquid whey)
- 2 cloves garlic, minced
- 1/2 cup chopped walnuts
- Salt, to taste
- Olive oil

- Optional: Mint leaves for garnish

Instructions:

Preheat the oven to 400°F (200°C).
Pierce the eggplants with a fork and roast them in the oven until the skin is charred, and the inside is soft.
Allow the eggplants to cool, peel off the skin, and mash the flesh.
In a pan, sauté minced garlic in olive oil until fragrant.
Add the mashed eggplant to the pan and cook for a few minutes, stirring well.
Stir in kashk and chopped walnuts. Continue cooking until the mixture thickens.
Season with salt to taste.
Transfer the Kashk-e Bademjan to a serving dish, drizzle with olive oil, and garnish with mint leaves if desired.
Serve it with flatbread or as a side dish.

Both Halim and Kashk-e Bademjan are delightful dishes with distinct flavors and textures, often enjoyed in Persian cuisine.

Kookoo Sabzi

Ingredients:

- 4 cups mixed fresh herbs (parsley, cilantro, dill, chives, and green onions), finely chopped
- 1 cup spinach, finely chopped
- 4 large eggs
- 1 teaspoon baking powder
- 2 tablespoons all-purpose flour
- 1 teaspoon turmeric
- Salt and pepper to taste
- Olive oil or vegetable oil for frying

Instructions:

Prepare Herbs:
- Wash and finely chop the mixed herbs (parsley, cilantro, dill, chives, and green onions) and spinach. Ensure they are well-drained.

Beat Eggs:
- In a large mixing bowl, beat the eggs.

Combine Ingredients:
- Add baking powder, all-purpose flour, and turmeric to the beaten eggs. Mix well until the ingredients are thoroughly combined.
- Incorporate the chopped herbs and spinach into the egg mixture. Mix until the herbs are evenly distributed.

Seasoning:
- Add salt and pepper to taste. Adjust the seasoning according to your preference.

Frying:
- Heat a few tablespoons of oil in a non-stick skillet over medium heat.
- Pour the herb and egg mixture into the skillet, spreading it evenly.

Cooking:
- Cook the Kookoo Sabzi on medium heat until the bottom is golden brown and the edges start to set.

Flip:
- Carefully flip the Kookoo Sabzi to cook the other side. You can use a plate to help with the flipping process.

Finish Cooking:
- Continue cooking until the other side is golden brown and the middle is fully set.

Serving:
- Slide the Kookoo Sabzi onto a serving plate and let it cool slightly before cutting it into wedges.

Garnish:
- Garnish with additional fresh herbs or radishes.

Serving:
- Serve Kookoo Sabzi warm or at room temperature. It's often enjoyed with flatbread or on its own.

Kookoo Sabzi is a delightful dish that highlights the vibrant flavors of fresh herbs. It is a staple during Persian New Year (Nowruz) celebrations and is a favorite in Iranian households throughout the year.

Laboo va Goje Farangi

Ingredients:

- 2 medium-sized beets, cooked, peeled, and diced
- 1 cup pomegranate arils
- 1/4 cup chopped fresh mint
- 1/4 cup chopped fresh parsley
- 2 tablespoons olive oil
- 1 tablespoon pomegranate molasses (optional)
- Salt and pepper to taste
- Crushed walnuts for garnish (optional)

Instructions:

Prepare Beets:
- Cook the beets until tender (you can boil, roast, or steam them). Once cooked, peel and dice them into bite-sized pieces.

Mix Ingredients:
- In a bowl, combine the diced beets, pomegranate arils, chopped mint, and chopped parsley.

Dressing:
- In a small bowl, whisk together olive oil and pomegranate molasses (if using) to make the dressing.

Combine and Season:
- Pour the dressing over the beet and pomegranate mixture and toss gently to combine.
- Season the salad with salt and pepper to taste.

Chill:
- Allow the salad to chill in the refrigerator for at least 30 minutes to let the flavors meld.

Garnish:
- Before serving, garnish with crushed walnuts if desired.

Serving:
- Serve the Laboo va Goje Farangi salad as a side dish or as part of a mezze platter.

This salad combines the earthy sweetness of beets with the juicy and tart burst of pomegranate arils, creating a vibrant and visually appealing dish. It's a delightful addition to Persian meals and provides a refreshing contrast to other flavors on the table.

Anar Mosamma

Ingredients:

- 1 cup walnuts, ground
- 1 large onion, finely chopped
- 500g chicken or duck, cut into pieces
- 1 cup pomegranate molasses
- 1 tablespoon sugar (optional, to balance the tartness)
- 2 tablespoons vegetable oil
- Salt and pepper to taste

Instructions:

Sauté Onion:
- In a large pot, sauté finely chopped onions in vegetable oil until golden brown.

Brown Meat:
- Add the chicken or duck pieces to the pot and brown them on all sides.

Ground Walnuts:
- Add the ground walnuts to the pot and stir well, ensuring the meat is coated.

Pomegranate Molasses:
- Pour in the pomegranate molasses and stir to combine.

Simmer:
- Add enough water to cover the meat, bring to a boil, then reduce the heat and let it simmer until the meat is tender and the sauce thickens.

Season:
- Season with salt and pepper. If the sauce is too tart, you can add sugar to balance the flavors.

Finish Cooking:
- Continue simmering until the oil separates and rises to the top, indicating that the Fesenjan is ready.

Serving:
- Serve Fesenjan over rice.

This dish is known for its unique combination of savory and sweet flavors, creating a rich and luxurious stew. Pomegranate molasses gives it a tangy and slightly sweet taste, while the ground walnuts add depth and creaminess to the sauce. Fesenjan is often enjoyed during special occasions in Persian cuisine.

Gondi

Ingredients:

For the Dumplings:

- 1 cup chickpea flour (besan)
- 1 cup ground chicken or turkey
- 1 medium onion, finely chopped
- 1/2 cup finely chopped fresh herbs (cilantro, parsley, dill)
- 1/4 cup vegetable oil
- 1 teaspoon ground turmeric
- 1 teaspoon ground cumin
- 1/2 teaspoon baking powder
- Salt and pepper to taste

For the Soup:

- 8 cups chicken or vegetable broth
- 1 large onion, finely chopped
- 2 cloves garlic, minced
- 1 tablespoon vegetable oil
- 1 teaspoon ground turmeric
- Salt and pepper to taste

Instructions:

Prepare Dumpling Mixture:
- In a large bowl, combine chickpea flour, ground chicken, finely chopped onion, fresh herbs, vegetable oil, ground turmeric, ground cumin, baking powder, salt, and pepper.
- Mix well until you have a homogenous mixture. It should be thick enough to form dumplings.

Shape Dumplings:
- Wet your hands, take a portion of the mixture, and shape it into small, round dumplings (about the size of a walnut). Repeat until all the mixture is used.

Prepare Soup:
- In a large pot, sauté finely chopped onion and minced garlic in vegetable oil until golden brown.
- Add ground turmeric and continue sautéing for a minute.

Cook Dumplings:
- Carefully place the shaped dumplings into the pot with sautéed onions and garlic.
- Pour in the chicken or vegetable broth, season with salt and pepper, and bring the soup to a gentle boil.

Simmer:
- Reduce the heat to low, cover the pot, and let the dumplings simmer for about 1 to 1.5 hours until they are cooked through and the soup thickens.

Adjust Seasoning:
- Taste and adjust the seasoning if necessary.

Serving:
- Serve Gondi hot in bowls, with the dumplings floating in the flavorful broth.

Gondi is a comfort food in Persian cuisine, and the combination of chickpea flour, ground meat, and aromatic spices creates a unique and satisfying dish. It is often enjoyed with flatbread or over rice.

Salad-e-Olivieh Miveh

Ingredients:

- 3 large potatoes, boiled, peeled, and diced
- 2 cups cooked chicken, shredded
- 1 cup peas, cooked
- 3 hard-boiled eggs, chopped
- 1 cup dill pickles, finely chopped
- 1 cup carrots, boiled and diced
- 1 cup canned corn, drained
- 1 cup mayonnaise
- 2 tablespoons sour cream
- 1 tablespoon Dijon mustard (optional)
- Salt and pepper to taste

Instructions:

In a large mixing bowl, combine the diced potatoes, shredded chicken, cooked peas, chopped eggs, pickles, boiled carrots, and corn.

In a separate bowl, mix mayonnaise, sour cream, Dijon mustard (if using), salt, and pepper. Adjust the seasoning to your taste.

Pour the dressing over the salad ingredients and gently toss until everything is well coated.

Chill the Olivieh Salad in the refrigerator for at least a couple of hours to allow the flavors to meld.

Before serving, check the seasoning and adjust if necessary. You can garnish with additional chopped dill pickles or herbs.

Serve the Olivieh Salad as a side dish or on its own. It's often enjoyed with bread or crackers.

Olivieh Salad is a popular dish in Iran and is often served during gatherings and celebrations. It's known for its creamy texture and a combination of flavors from the vegetables, chicken, and tangy dressing.

Havij Polo Ba Mahicheh

Ingredients:

For the Rice:

- 2 cups basmati rice
- 4 large carrots, julienned
- 1 large onion, thinly sliced
- 1/2 cup raisins (optional)
- 1/4 cup oil (vegetable or olive oil)
- 1/2 teaspoon ground cinnamon
- Salt and pepper to taste

For the Lamb Shanks:

- 4 lamb shanks
- 1 large onion, chopped
- 3 cloves garlic, minced
- 2 tablespoons tomato paste
- 1 teaspoon ground turmeric
- 1 teaspoon ground cumin
- 1 teaspoon ground coriander
- 1 teaspoon ground cinnamon
- Salt and pepper to taste
- 2 cups water or beef broth

Instructions:

Prepare the Lamb Shanks:
- In a large pot, sauté chopped onions and minced garlic in oil until golden brown.
- Add lamb shanks to the pot and brown on all sides.
- Stir in tomato paste, ground turmeric, cumin, coriander, cinnamon, salt, and pepper. Mix well to coat the lamb shanks with the spices.
- Pour in water or beef broth, cover the pot, and let it simmer over low heat until the lamb is tender and cooked through. This may take 1.5 to 2 hours.

Prepare the Carrot Rice:
- Wash the basmati rice under cold water until the water runs clear. Soak the rice in water for about 30 minutes.

- In a separate pan, sauté thinly sliced onions in oil until golden.
- Add julienned carrots to the pan and continue sautéing until the carrots are slightly caramelized.
- Drain the soaked rice and add it to the pan. Stir in ground cinnamon, salt, and pepper. Mix well to combine.
- Add raisins if using.

Layering:
- In a large pot, layer the bottom with a portion of the carrot and rice mixture.
- Place the cooked lamb shanks on top of the rice.
- Cover the lamb shanks with the remaining carrot and rice mixture.

Steam:
- Cover the pot with a clean kitchen towel and then the lid. Steam the rice over low heat for about 45 minutes to 1 hour until the rice is cooked and fluffy.

Serving:
- Gently fluff the rice with a fork and serve Havij Polo Ba Mahicheh hot. You can serve it on a platter with the lamb shanks on top.

This dish is a celebration of flavors and textures, combining the sweetness of carrots, the fragrance of basmati rice, and the richness of lamb shanks. It's a classic in Persian cuisine and is often served during special occasions and gatherings.

Dough

Ingredients:

- 2 cups plain yogurt
- 2 cups cold water
- 1/2 cup ice cubes (optional)
- 1 cucumber, finely diced
- 2 tablespoons dried mint
- Salt to taste

Instructions:

In a large mixing bowl, whisk the yogurt until smooth.
Add cold water to the yogurt and continue whisking until well combined.
If using, add ice cubes to the mixture to chill it.
Finely dice the cucumber and add it to the yogurt-water mixture.
Sprinkle dried mint over the mixture. You can adjust the amount of mint according to your preference.
Season the Doogh with salt to taste. Start with a small amount and adjust as needed.
Continue whisking the mixture to ensure all the ingredients are well incorporated.
Refrigerate the Doogh for at least 30 minutes before serving to allow the flavors to meld.
Before serving, give the Doogh a final stir and pour it into glasses.
Optionally, garnish with a mint leaf or a slice of cucumber on top.

Doogh is often served as a refreshing accompaniment to meals, especially during the hot summer months. It complements various Persian dishes and is a popular choice for breaking the fast during the month of Ramadan. The combination of yogurt, water, cucumber, and mint creates a cool and tangy beverage that is both hydrating and flavorful.

Nan-e-Barbari Ba Paneer

Ingredients:

For Barbari Bread:

- 4 cups all-purpose flour
- 2 teaspoons active dry yeast
- 1 teaspoon sugar
- 2 teaspoons salt
- 1 1/2 cups warm water
- Nigella seeds or sesame seeds for topping (optional)

For Paneer Filling:

- 1 cup paneer, crumbled or grated
- Fresh herbs (such as mint or cilantro), chopped
- Olive oil
- Salt and pepper to taste

Instructions:

Prepare the Barbari Bread Dough:
- In a bowl, dissolve sugar in warm water. Sprinkle active dry yeast over the water and let it sit for about 5-10 minutes until it becomes frothy.
- In a large mixing bowl, combine flour and salt. Make a well in the center and pour in the yeast mixture.
- Mix the ingredients to form a dough. Knead the dough on a floured surface for about 8-10 minutes until it becomes smooth and elastic.
- Place the dough in a lightly oiled bowl, cover it with a damp cloth, and let it rise in a warm place for 1-2 hours or until doubled in size.

Preheat the Oven:
- Preheat your oven to a high temperature (around 450°F or 230°C).

Prepare the Paneer Filling:
- In a bowl, combine crumbled or grated paneer with chopped fresh herbs. Season with salt and pepper. Drizzle with a bit of olive oil and mix well.

Shape and Top the Barbari Bread:
- Divide the risen dough into two portions. Roll each portion into a rectangular or oval shape on a floured surface.
- Transfer the rolled dough to a baking sheet.

- Spread the paneer filling evenly over the surface of each bread.
- If desired, sprinkle nigella seeds or sesame seeds on top for added flavor and appearance.

Bake:
- Place the baking sheet in the preheated oven and bake for about 15-20 minutes or until the bread is golden brown and cooked through.

Serve:
- Once baked, remove the Barbari bread from the oven and let it cool for a few minutes.
- Slice and serve the Barbari Bread with Paneer while it's still warm.

This Barbari bread with paneer is a delightful combination of the chewy texture of the bread and the creamy, flavorful paneer filling. It makes for a great accompaniment to various Persian dishes or can be enjoyed on its own.

Aash-e Reshteh

Ingredients:

- 1 cup lentils, washed and drained
- 1 cup chickpeas, soaked overnight
- 1 cup red kidney beans, soaked overnight
- 1 cup chopped leeks or green onions
- 1 cup chopped spinach
- 1 cup chopped parsley
- 1 cup chopped cilantro
- 1 cup chopped dill
- 1 cup Persian noodles (Reshteh) or linguine, broken into short pieces
- 1 large onion, finely chopped
- 4 cloves garlic, minced
- 2 tablespoons vegetable oil
- 2 tablespoons dried mint (for garnish)
- 1 teaspoon ground turmeric
- Salt and pepper to taste
- Yogurt (optional, for serving)

Instructions:

Prepare the Legumes:
- In a large pot, combine lentils, chickpeas, and red kidney beans. Add enough water to cover the legumes and bring to a boil. Simmer until the legumes are cooked through.

Sauté Aromatics:
- In a separate pan, sauté chopped onions in vegetable oil until golden brown. Add minced garlic and ground turmeric, and continue sautéing for another minute.

Add Aromatics to Legumes:
- Add the sautéed onion mixture to the pot with the cooked legumes.

Add Vegetables and Noodles:
- Add chopped leeks, spinach, parsley, cilantro, and dill to the pot. Stir well.
- Add Persian noodles or broken linguine to the pot. Cook until the noodles are tender.

Season:

- Season the soup with salt and pepper to taste. Adjust the seasoning according to your preference.

Simmer:
- Allow the soup to simmer for an additional 15-20 minutes to let the flavors meld.

Prepare Mint Garnish:
- In a small pan, heat dried mint until fragrant. This will be used as a garnish.

Serving:
- Ladle Aash-e Reshteh into bowls. Top each serving with a sprinkle of dried mint.

Optional:
- Serve Aash-e Reshteh with a dollop of yogurt on top, if desired.

Aash-e Reshteh is a comforting and nutritious soup that is often enjoyed with family and friends. The combination of legumes, herbs, and noodles creates a delicious and satisfying dish that is deeply rooted in Persian culinary tradition.

Kuku Sibzamini

Ingredients:

- 4 large baking potatoes
- 1 cup ground beef or lamb
- 1 onion, finely chopped
- 2 cloves garlic, minced
- 1 teaspoon ground cumin
- 1 teaspoon ground coriander
- Salt and pepper to taste
- 1/2 cup chopped fresh herbs (parsley, cilantro, dill)
- 4 eggs
- Olive oil for cooking
- Optional: Greek yogurt or labneh for serving

Instructions:

Prepare Potatoes:
- Preheat the oven to 400°F (200°C).
- Wash and scrub the potatoes. Prick them with a fork and bake in the oven until they are tender, about 45-60 minutes.

Prepare Filling:
- In a pan, sauté chopped onions in olive oil until translucent. Add minced garlic and continue cooking for a minute.
- Add ground beef or lamb to the pan and cook until browned.
- Season the meat with ground cumin, ground coriander, salt, and pepper. Stir in the chopped fresh herbs and cook for a few more minutes.

Prepare Potatoes for Stuffing:
- Once the potatoes are baked and slightly cooled, cut off the tops and scoop out the insides, leaving a thin layer to create a potato shell.

Stuff the Potatoes:
- Fill each potato shell with the cooked meat mixture.

Bake Again:
- Place the stuffed potatoes back in the oven for about 10-15 minutes or until the filling is heated through.

Prepare Kuku Mixture:
- In a bowl, beat the eggs and season with salt and pepper.

Cook Kuku Mixture:

- Pour the beaten eggs over the stuffed potatoes, making sure the filling is well covered.
- Return to the oven and bake until the eggs are set and slightly golden.

Serve:
- Serve the Kuku Sibzamini-inspired dish hot.
- Optionally, serve with a dollop of Greek yogurt or labneh on the side.

This recipe combines the concept of a stuffed potato with a Kuku-inspired egg topping, resulting in a flavorful and hearty dish. Adjust the ingredients and seasonings to suit your taste preferences.

Moraba Sabz

Ingredients:

- 2 pounds (about 1 kg) unripe green plums (gojeh sabz)
- 4 cups granulated sugar
- 2 cups water
- Juice of 1-2 lemons (optional, for added tartness)

Instructions:

Prepare Green Plums:
- Wash the green plums thoroughly. Remove the stems and any blemishes. Prick each plum with a fork or make a small slit to allow the syrup to penetrate.

Make Sugar Syrup:
- In a large pot, combine sugar and water. Heat over medium heat, stirring until the sugar dissolves.

Add Green Plums:
- Add the washed and prepared green plums to the sugar syrup. Stir gently to coat the plums.

Cooking:
- Bring the mixture to a boil, then reduce the heat to a simmer. Cook the green plums in the syrup until they become tender and the syrup thickens. This may take about 1 to 1.5 hours.

Optional Lemon Juice:
- If you prefer a more tart flavor, squeeze the juice of 1-2 lemons and add it to the jam during the last 15-20 minutes of cooking.

Test for Doneness:
- To check if the jam is ready, place a small amount on a cold plate. If it sets and wrinkles when touched, it's done.

Cooling and Jarring:
- Once the Moraba Sabz is ready, remove it from heat and let it cool slightly.
- Ladle the jam into sterilized jars and seal them.

Storage:
- Store the sealed jars in a cool, dark place. Once opened, keep the jam refrigerated.

Moraba Sabz is traditionally enjoyed with flatbread, as a condiment, or as a sweet topping for breakfast items. The green plums provide a unique tartness to the jam, and the process of making it is a cherished part of Persian culinary traditions.

Ash-e Jow

Ingredients:

- 1 cup pearl barley, washed and soaked overnight
- 1 cup yellow split peas, washed
- 1 large onion, finely chopped
- 2 cloves garlic, minced
- 2 medium-sized carrots, diced
- 2 celery stalks, diced
- 1 cup chopped leeks or green onions
- 1 cup chopped fresh herbs (a combination of parsley, cilantro, and dill)
- 1 teaspoon turmeric
- 1 teaspoon ground cumin
- 1 teaspoon ground coriander
- Salt and pepper to taste
- 8 cups vegetable or chicken broth
- 2 tablespoons vegetable oil
- Juice of 1-2 lemons (optional, for serving)
- Greek yogurt or kashk (fermented whey) for garnish

Instructions:

Prepare Barley and Split Peas:
- Wash and soak the pearl barley overnight. Rinse the yellow split peas.

Sauté Aromatics:
- In a large pot, heat vegetable oil over medium heat. Sauté chopped onions until golden brown.
- Add minced garlic, ground turmeric, ground cumin, and ground coriander. Sauté for an additional 2-3 minutes.

Add Vegetables:
- Add diced carrots, celery, and chopped leeks or green onions to the pot. Cook for about 5 minutes until the vegetables start to soften.

Add Barley and Split Peas:
- Drain and add the soaked pearl barley and rinsed yellow split peas to the pot. Stir to combine.

Pour Broth:
- Pour vegetable or chicken broth into the pot. Bring the soup to a boil, then reduce the heat to a simmer.

Cooking:

- Simmer the soup, covered, for about 1 to 1.5 hours or until the barley and split peas are tender. Stir occasionally.

Add Fresh Herbs:
- Add chopped fresh herbs (parsley, cilantro, and dill) to the soup during the last 10-15 minutes of cooking.

Season:
- Season the soup with salt and pepper to taste. Adjust the seasoning according to your preference.

Serving:
- Ladle the Ash-e Jow into bowls. Optionally, squeeze fresh lemon juice over each serving.

Garnish:
- Garnish each bowl with a dollop of Greek yogurt or kashk.

Ash-e Jow is typically served hot and can be enjoyed as a comforting meal on its own or with flatbread. The combination of barley, split peas, and a variety of vegetables creates a nourishing and flavorful soup in Persian cuisine.

Kalam Polo Ba Mahicheh

Ingredients:

For the Rice:

- 2 cups Basmati rice
- 1 medium-sized cabbage, finely shredded
- 1 large onion, finely chopped
- 1/4 cup vegetable oil or ghee
- 1 teaspoon ground turmeric
- Salt and pepper to taste

For the Lamb Shanks:

- 4 lamb shanks
- 1 large onion, chopped
- 3 cloves garlic, minced
- 2 tablespoons tomato paste
- 1 teaspoon ground turmeric
- 1 teaspoon ground cumin
- 1 teaspoon ground coriander
- 1 teaspoon ground cinnamon
- Salt and pepper to taste
- 2 cups water or lamb broth

Instructions:

Prepare Lamb Shanks:
- In a large pot, sauté chopped onions in oil until golden brown.
- Add minced garlic and continue sautéing for a minute.
- Add lamb shanks to the pot and brown them on all sides.
- Stir in tomato paste, ground turmeric, cumin, coriander, cinnamon, salt, and pepper. Mix well to coat the lamb shanks with the spices.
- Pour in water or lamb broth, cover the pot, and let it simmer over low heat until the lamb is tender and cooked through. This may take 1.5 to 2 hours.

Prepare Rice:

- Wash Basmati rice under cold water until the water runs clear. Soak the rice in water for about 30 minutes.
- In a large pot, sauté finely chopped onions in oil or ghee until golden brown.
- Add finely shredded cabbage to the pot and sauté until it softens.
- Stir in ground turmeric, salt, and pepper.

Cook Rice:
- Drain the soaked rice and add it to the pot with sautéed cabbage. Mix well.
- Place the lamb shanks on top of the rice and cabbage mixture.
- Add 1/2 cup of water from the lamb shank pot to the rice pot. This will help the rice cook and absorb the flavors.

Simmer:
- Cover the pot with a clean kitchen towel and then the lid. Simmer the rice over low heat for about 45 minutes to 1 hour until the rice is cooked and fluffy.

Serve:
- Once the rice is cooked, fluff it with a fork and serve it on a platter with the lamb shanks on top.

Kalam Polo Ba Mahicheh is a delicious and aromatic dish that brings together the earthy flavors of cabbage, the richness of lamb shanks, and the fragrant spices. It's often enjoyed with a side of yogurt or a fresh salad.

Maast-o-Khiar-o-Anar

Ingredients:

- 2 cups Greek yogurt
- 1 cucumber, finely diced or grated
- 1/2 cup pomegranate seeds
- 2 tablespoons fresh mint, chopped
- 2 cloves garlic, minced
- 1 tablespoon dried mint (optional)
- Salt to taste
- Black pepper to taste
- Olive oil for drizzling (optional)

Instructions:

Prepare Cucumber:
- If using a fresh cucumber, peel and finely dice or grate it. If the cucumber has a lot of water, you can squeeze out the excess liquid.

Mix Yogurt:
- In a mixing bowl, combine Greek yogurt with the diced or grated cucumber.

Add Pomegranate Seeds and Herbs:
- Gently fold in the pomegranate seeds, fresh chopped mint, minced garlic, and dried mint (if using).

Season:
- Season the mixture with salt and black pepper to taste. Adjust the seasoning according to your preference.

Chill:
- Cover the bowl and let the Maast-o-Khiar-o-Anar chill in the refrigerator for at least 30 minutes to allow the flavors to meld.

Serve:
- Before serving, give the mixture a gentle stir. Optionally, drizzle a bit of olive oil on top for added richness.

Garnish:
- Garnish with additional pomegranate seeds and fresh mint before serving.

Enjoy:
- Serve Maast-o-Khiar-o-Anar as a refreshing side dish or dip with bread, crackers, or as an accompaniment to Persian main courses.

This dish is known for its combination of creamy yogurt, crunchy cucumber, and the burst of sweetness from pomegranate seeds. It adds a cool and refreshing element to meals and is particularly popular during warm weather.

Khoresh-e Bamiyeh

Ingredients:

- 1 pound (about 500g) okra, washed and trimmed
- 1 pound beef or lamb stew meat, cut into chunks
- 1 large onion, finely chopped
- 2 cloves garlic, minced
- 3 ripe tomatoes, peeled and chopped (or 1 can of crushed tomatoes)
- 2 tablespoons tomato paste
- 1 teaspoon ground turmeric
- 1 teaspoon ground cumin
- 1 teaspoon ground coriander
- Salt and pepper to taste
- 2 tablespoons vegetable oil
- 1 tablespoon dried lime powder (optional)
- Fresh lemon juice (optional, for serving)
- Cooked rice for serving

Instructions:

Prepare Okra:
- Trim the ends of the okra and cut them into 1-inch pieces. If using frozen okra, thaw and pat dry.

Sear the Meat:
- In a large pot, heat vegetable oil over medium heat. Add the meat chunks and sear until browned on all sides.

Add Aromatics:
- Add chopped onions to the pot and sauté until golden brown. Add minced garlic and sauté for an additional minute.

Add Tomatoes and Spices:
- Add chopped tomatoes, tomato paste, ground turmeric, ground cumin, and ground coriander to the pot. Stir well to combine.

Cook the Meat:
- Pour in enough water to cover the meat and bring the mixture to a boil. Reduce the heat, cover, and simmer until the meat is tender. This may take about 1.5 to 2 hours.

Add Okra:

- Once the meat is tender, add the okra to the pot. If using dried lime powder, add it at this stage. Stir gently to combine.

Simmer:
- Continue simmering the stew until the okra is cooked and tender. This usually takes about 30-40 minutes.

Adjust Seasoning:
- Season the stew with salt and pepper to taste. Adjust the seasoning according to your preference.

Serve:
- Serve Khoresh-e Bamiyeh over a bed of cooked rice. Optionally, squeeze fresh lemon juice over each serving.

Khoresh-e Bamiyeh is a flavorful and hearty dish that showcases the unique texture of okra. The combination of spices and slow cooking allows the flavors to meld, resulting in a delicious stew that is commonly enjoyed in Persian cuisine.

Baghali Polo Ba Mahicheh

Ingredients:

For the Rice:

- 2 cups Basmati rice
- 2 cups fresh or frozen lima beans (baghali), thawed if frozen
- 1 large onion, thinly sliced
- 1/2 cup chopped fresh dill
- 1/4 cup vegetable oil or ghee
- 1 teaspoon ground cumin
- Salt and pepper to taste

For the Lamb Shanks:

- 4 lamb shanks
- 1 large onion, chopped
- 3 cloves garlic, minced
- 2 tablespoons tomato paste
- 1 teaspoon ground turmeric
- 1 teaspoon ground cinnamon
- Salt and pepper to taste
- 2 cups water or lamb broth
- Vegetable oil for cooking

Instructions:

Prepare the Rice:
- Wash the Basmati rice under cold water until the water runs clear. Soak the rice in water for about 30 minutes.
- In a pot, bring water to a boil and add salt. Add the soaked and drained rice to the boiling water. Cook until the rice is parboiled (partially cooked) but still has a bite to it. Drain the rice.

Sauté Onion and Lima Beans:
- In a pan, sauté thinly sliced onions in vegetable oil or ghee until golden brown. Add chopped fresh dill and ground cumin. Stir for a minute.
- Add lima beans to the pan and sauté for a few more minutes.

Layer Rice and Lima Bean Mixture:
- In the pot, layer half of the parboiled rice, followed by half of the lima bean mixture. Repeat the layers, finishing with a layer of rice on top.

Create Steam Holes:
- Using the back of a wooden spoon, make a few holes in the rice to allow steam to escape during cooking.

Cook the Rice:
- Cover the pot with a clean kitchen towel and then the lid. Cook the rice over low heat for about 45 minutes to 1 hour, allowing it to steam and fully cook.

Prepare Lamb Shanks:
- In a separate pot, sauté chopped onions in vegetable oil until golden brown.
- Add minced garlic and sauté for an additional minute.
- Add lamb shanks to the pot and brown them on all sides.
- Stir in tomato paste, ground turmeric, ground cinnamon, salt, and pepper. Mix well to coat the lamb shanks with the spices.
- Pour in water or lamb broth, cover the pot, and let it simmer over low heat until the lamb is tender and cooked through. This may take 1.5 to 2 hours.

Serve:
- Once the rice and lamb are ready, serve the Baghali Polo Ba Mahicheh by placing a portion of rice on a platter and arranging lamb shanks on top.

Enjoy:
- Garnish with additional dill or saffron if desired. Serve and enjoy this flavorful Persian dish.

Baghali Polo Ba Mahicheh is a celebration of flavors, combining the aromatic dill-infused rice with the tender and spiced lamb shanks. It's a popular choice for gatherings and special occasions in Persian cuisine.

Sambuseh

Ingredients:

For the Dough:

- 2 cups all-purpose flour
- 1/2 cup vegetable oil or melted butter
- 1/2 cup water
- 1/2 teaspoon salt

For the Filling:

- 2 large potatoes, boiled and mashed
- 1 cup cooked and drained lentils
- 1 cup frozen peas
- 1 large onion, finely chopped
- 2 cloves garlic, minced
- 1 teaspoon ground cumin
- 1 teaspoon ground coriander
- 1/2 teaspoon turmeric
- Salt and pepper to taste
- Vegetable oil for frying

Instructions:

Prepare the Dough:
- In a bowl, combine the flour, salt, and oil (or melted butter).
- Gradually add water and knead until you have a smooth and elastic dough. Cover and let it rest for 30 minutes.

Prepare the Filling:
- In a pan, heat a bit of oil and sauté chopped onions until translucent.
- Add minced garlic and cook for an additional minute.
- Add mashed potatoes, cooked lentils, frozen peas, ground cumin, ground coriander, turmeric, salt, and pepper. Mix well and cook until the filling is heated through. Adjust seasoning to taste.

Assemble and Shape:

- Divide the dough into small balls. Roll each ball into a thin circle (about 6 inches in diameter).
- Place a portion of the filling in the center of each circle.

Fold and Seal:
- Fold the dough over the filling to create a half-moon shape. Press the edges to seal, either by crimping with a fork or by twisting and folding the edges.

Fry:
- Heat vegetable oil in a deep pan. Fry the sambuseh in batches until they are golden brown and crispy.

Drain and Serve:
- Remove the sambuseh with a slotted spoon and place them on a paper towel to drain excess oil.

Serve:
- Serve the sambuseh warm, either on its own or with chutney or yogurt for dipping.

Sambuseh is a delicious snack or appetizer enjoyed in various cultures. The filling and spices can be adjusted based on personal preferences, making it a versatile and delightful dish.

Khoresh-e Beh

Ingredients:

- 4 quinces, peeled, cored, and sliced into wedges
- 1.5 pounds (about 700g) meat (lamb or beef), cubed
- 1 large onion, finely chopped
- 2 tablespoons tomato paste
- 1 cup yellow split peas, soaked
- 2 teaspoons ground cinnamon
- 1 teaspoon ground turmeric
- 1/2 teaspoon ground saffron (optional)
- Salt and pepper to taste
- Vegetable oil for cooking
- 2 tablespoons sugar (optional, to balance tartness)

Instructions:

Prepare Quinces:
- Peel, core, and slice quinces into wedges. If quinces are too tart, you can soak them in water with a bit of salt to reduce the tartness.

Sauté Onions:
- In a large pot, heat vegetable oil over medium heat. Sauté chopped onions until golden brown.

Brown Meat:
- Add cubed meat to the pot and brown it on all sides.

Add Spices and Tomato Paste:
- Stir in ground cinnamon, ground turmeric, and tomato paste. Mix well to coat the meat with spices.

Add Split Peas:
- Drain the soaked yellow split peas and add them to the pot. Mix with the meat and spices.

Pour Water:
- Pour enough water into the pot to cover the meat and split peas. Bring to a boil, then reduce the heat to simmer.

Cook until Tender:
- Allow the meat and split peas to simmer until they are partially cooked, which may take about 1 to 1.5 hours.

Add Quinces:

- Add the sliced quinces to the pot. Continue cooking until both the meat and quinces are tender. Adjust the seasoning to taste.

Optional Sugar:
- If the quinces are still too tart, you can add sugar to balance the flavors. Adjust the sweetness according to your preference.

Optional Saffron:
- If using saffron, dissolve it in a bit of warm water and add it to the stew.

Simmer:
- Let the stew simmer for an additional 15-20 minutes, allowing all the flavors to meld.

Serve:
- Serve Khoresh-e Beh over rice or with flatbread.

Khoresh-e Beh is known for its sweet and sour flavor profile, with the quinces adding a unique and aromatic touch to the stew. It's a delightful dish often enjoyed during the fall when quinces are in season.

Bastani Sonnati

Ingredients:

- 2 cups heavy cream
- 1 cup whole milk
- 1 cup sugar
- 1/2 teaspoon ground saffron threads (dissolved in a tablespoon of hot water)
- 1/4 cup rosewater
- 1/2 cup chopped pistachios (unsalted)
- 1/4 cup crushed frozen or dried edible rose petals (optional)
- 1/4 teaspoon ground cardamom (optional)

Instructions:

Infuse Saffron:
- Dissolve ground saffron in a tablespoon of hot water and let it steep to release its color and flavor.

Prepare the Base:
- In a saucepan, heat the heavy cream and whole milk over medium heat until it begins to simmer. Stir frequently to avoid scalding.

Add Sugar:
- Once the milk and cream are heated, add sugar to the mixture. Stir until the sugar is completely dissolved.

Add Saffron and Rosewater:
- Add the saffron infusion and rosewater to the milk mixture. Stir well to combine.

Cool the Mixture:
- Allow the mixture to cool to room temperature, and then refrigerate it for at least 4 hours or overnight to chill thoroughly.

Churn the Ice Cream:
- Pour the chilled mixture into an ice cream maker and churn according to the manufacturer's instructions until it reaches a soft-serve consistency.

Add Pistachios and Rose Petals:
- During the last few minutes of churning, add chopped pistachios and crushed rose petals (if using). This adds texture and flavor to the ice cream.

Transfer and Freeze:

- Transfer the churned ice cream to a lidded container. Smooth the top and cover with a piece of parchment paper or plastic wrap to prevent ice crystals from forming.

Optional Cardamom Garnish:
- If desired, sprinkle a small amount of ground cardamom over the top for extra flavor.

Freeze until Firm:
- Freeze the ice cream for several hours or until it reaches a firm consistency.

Serve:
- Scoop Bastani Sonnati into bowls or cones and enjoy the rich, saffron-infused goodness.

Bastani Sonnati is often enjoyed on its own or served alongside Persian desserts like Faloodeh. Its unique blend of saffron and rosewater makes it a distinctive and delightful treat.

Khoresht-e Havij Ba Gosht

Ingredients:

- 1 pound (about 500g) stewing meat (lamb or beef), cut into cubes
- 1 large onion, finely chopped
- 4-5 large carrots, peeled and sliced
- 2 tablespoons tomato paste
- 1 teaspoon ground turmeric
- 1 teaspoon ground cinnamon
- Salt and pepper to taste
- Vegetable oil for cooking
- 2 cups water or beef broth
- 1 tablespoon lime or lemon juice (optional, for a hint of acidity)
- 2 tablespoons chopped fresh parsley or cilantro (for garnish)
- Steamed rice for serving

Instructions:

Sauté Onions:
- In a pot, heat a few tablespoons of vegetable oil over medium heat. Sauté chopped onions until they become golden brown.

Brown the Meat:
- Add the cubed stewing meat to the pot. Brown the meat on all sides to seal in the flavors.

Add Spices:
- Stir in ground turmeric, ground cinnamon, salt, and pepper. Mix well to coat the meat with the spices.

Add Tomato Paste:
- Add tomato paste to the pot and continue stirring for a couple of minutes to incorporate it into the mixture.

Cook Carrots:
- Add the sliced carrots to the pot and mix with the meat and spices.

Pour Water or Broth:
- Pour water or beef broth into the pot, ensuring that the ingredients are fully covered.

Simmer:

- Bring the stew to a boil, then reduce the heat to low, cover the pot, and let it simmer for about 1.5 to 2 hours or until the meat is tender and the flavors meld.

Adjust Seasoning:
- Taste the stew and adjust the seasoning if needed. If you prefer a hint of acidity, you can add lime or lemon juice.

Garnish:
- Just before serving, garnish the Khoresht-e Havij Ba Gosht with chopped fresh parsley or cilantro.

Serve:
- Serve the carrot stew over steamed rice.

Khoresht-e Havij Ba Gosht is a comforting and aromatic Persian stew with the sweetness of carrots complementing the savory meat and spices. It's often enjoyed with rice and a side of yogurt.

Zeytoon Parvardeh Va Panir

Ingredients:

- 1 cup green or black olives, pitted
- 1 cup walnuts, finely chopped or ground
- 2 tablespoons pomegranate molasses
- 2 cloves garlic, minced
- 1 tablespoon fresh mint, chopped
- 1 tablespoon fresh parsley, chopped
- 1 tablespoon olive oil
- Feta cheese or Persian white cheese (Panir) for serving
- Pomegranate seeds for garnish (optional)

Instructions:

Prepare the Marinade:
- In a bowl, combine chopped walnuts, pomegranate molasses, minced garlic, chopped mint, chopped parsley, and olive oil. Mix well to form a thick and flavorful marinade.

Marinate Olives:
- Add the pitted olives to the marinade, ensuring they are well coated. Allow them to marinate for at least 1-2 hours to absorb the flavors.

Serve with Cheese:
- Arrange the marinated olives on a serving plate along with pieces of Feta cheese or Persian white cheese (Panir).

Garnish (Optional):
- Optionally, garnish with additional chopped herbs or pomegranate seeds for a pop of color and extra freshness.

Serve:
- Serve Zeytoon Parvardeh Va Panir as an appetizer or side dish. It's often enjoyed with flatbread or crackers.

This dish offers a harmonious blend of salty olives, the earthy richness of walnuts, the tangy sweetness of pomegranate molasses, and the creaminess of cheese. It's a flavorful and visually appealing addition to your table, perfect for gatherings or as part of a Persian-inspired spread.

Khoresh-e Albaloo

Ingredients:

- 1 pound (about 500g) sour cherries, pitted
- 1.5 pounds (about 700g) stewing meat (lamb or beef), cut into cubes
- 1 large onion, finely chopped
- 2 tablespoons tomato paste
- 1 teaspoon ground turmeric
- 1 teaspoon ground cinnamon
- Salt and pepper to taste
- Vegetable oil for cooking
- 1-2 tablespoons sugar (optional, depending on the tartness of cherries)
- 1-2 tablespoons lime or lemon juice (optional, for extra acidity)
- Steamed rice for serving

Instructions:

Prepare Sour Cherries:
- If using fresh sour cherries, pit them. If using canned or frozen cherries, ensure they are drained.

Sauté Onions:
- In a pot, heat a few tablespoons of vegetable oil over medium heat. Sauté chopped onions until they become golden brown.

Brown the Meat:
- Add the cubed stewing meat to the pot. Brown the meat on all sides to seal in the flavors.

Add Spices:
- Stir in ground turmeric, ground cinnamon, salt, and pepper. Mix well to coat the meat with the spices.

Add Tomato Paste:
- Add tomato paste to the pot and continue stirring for a couple of minutes to incorporate it into the mixture.

Cook Cherries:
- Add the pitted sour cherries to the pot. If using canned or frozen cherries, make sure they are well-drained.

Pour Water:
- Pour enough water into the pot to cover the meat and cherries. Bring the stew to a boil.

Simmer:
- Reduce the heat to low, cover the pot, and let the stew simmer for about 1.5 to 2 hours or until the meat is tender and the flavors meld.

Adjust Sweetness and Acidity:
- Taste the stew and adjust the sweetness by adding sugar if needed. If you prefer more acidity, you can add lime or lemon juice.

Serve:
- Serve Khoresh-e Albaloo over steamed rice.

Khoresh-e Albaloo is known for its unique combination of savory and tart flavors, creating a delicious and comforting dish. The sweetness from the cherries, combined with the savory meat and spices, makes it a delightful choice, especially during the cherry season.

Maast-o-Khiar-o-Khiarshoor

Ingredients:

- 2 cups Greek yogurt
- 1 cucumber, finely diced or grated
- 3 Persian cucumbers (Khiarshoor), finely diced
- 2 cloves garlic, minced
- 2 tablespoons fresh mint, chopped
- 1 tablespoon dried mint (optional)
- Salt to taste
- Black pepper to taste
- Olive oil for drizzling (optional)

Instructions:

Prepare Cucumbers:
- If using regular cucumber, peel, and finely dice or grate it. For Persian cucumbers (Khiarshoor), finely dice them. If the cucumbers have a lot of water, you can squeeze out the excess liquid.

Mix Yogurt:
- In a mixing bowl, combine Greek yogurt with the diced or grated cucumber and diced Persian cucumbers.

Add Garlic and Herbs:
- Add minced garlic, fresh chopped mint, and dried mint (if using) to the yogurt mixture.

Season:
- Season the mixture with salt and black pepper to taste. Adjust the seasoning according to your preference.

Chill:
- Cover the bowl and let Maast-o-Khiar-o-Khiarshoor chill in the refrigerator for at least 30 minutes to allow the flavors to meld.

Serve:
- Before serving, give the mixture a gentle stir. Optionally, drizzle a bit of olive oil on top for added richness.

Garnish:
- Garnish with additional fresh mint before serving.

Enjoy:
- Serve Maast-o-Khiar-o-Khiarshoor as a refreshing side dish or dip with bread, crackers, or as an accompaniment to Persian main courses.

This dish is known for its combination of creamy yogurt, crunchy cucumber, and the unique flavor of Persian cucumbers. It adds a cool and refreshing element to meals and is particularly popular during warm weather.

Nan-e-Barbari Ba Paneer-o-Sabzi

Ingredients:

- 1 batch of Barbari bread (you can find ready-made Barbari bread or make it from scratch)
- Persian white cheese (Paneer), sliced or crumbled
- Fresh herbs (Sabzi) such as mint, basil, tarragon, and green onions, washed and chopped
- Radishes, washed and thinly sliced
- Cherry tomatoes, washed and halved
- Extra virgin olive oil for drizzling
- Salt and black pepper to taste

Instructions:

Prepare Barbari Bread:
- Either purchase Barbari bread from a Persian bakery or make it at home following a Barbari bread recipe.

Slice or Crumble Paneer:
- Slice or crumble Persian white cheese (Paneer) according to your preference.

Prepare Fresh Herbs:
- Wash and chop a variety of fresh herbs such as mint, basil, tarragon, and green onions.

Slice Vegetables:
- Thinly slice radishes and halve cherry tomatoes.

Assemble:
- Place slices or crumbles of paneer on the Barbari bread. Scatter chopped herbs, sliced radishes, and halved cherry tomatoes over the cheese.

Drizzle with Olive Oil:
- Drizzle extra virgin olive oil over the assembled Barbari bread, cheese, and herbs.

Season:
- Sprinkle salt and black pepper to taste.

Serve:
- Serve the Nan-e-Barbari Ba Paneer-o-Sabzi immediately. It's delicious when fresh and warm.

This dish is a delightful combination of textures and flavors—the crispy Barbari bread, creamy paneer, and the freshness of herbs and vegetables. It can be enjoyed as a light meal or a snack, perfect for gatherings or as part of a Persian-inspired feast.

Shirazi Omelette

Ingredients:

- 3 large eggs
- 1 small onion, finely chopped
- 1 tomato, diced
- 1/4 cup fresh parsley, chopped
- 1/4 cup fresh mint, chopped
- 1/4 cup Persian cucumber (Khiarshoor), finely diced
- Feta cheese, crumbled (optional)
- Salt and pepper to taste
- Olive oil or butter for cooking

Instructions:

Prepare Ingredients:
- Finely chop the onion, dice the tomato, chop the fresh parsley and mint, and finely dice the Persian cucumber.

Whisk Eggs:
- In a bowl, whisk the eggs until well combined. Season with salt and pepper.

Sauté Vegetables:
- In a non-stick skillet, heat a bit of olive oil or butter over medium heat. Sauté the chopped onion until softened.

Add Tomatoes and Cucumber:
- Add the diced tomatoes and Persian cucumber to the skillet. Cook for a few minutes until the vegetables are softened.

Pour Whisked Eggs:
- Pour the whisked eggs over the sautéed vegetables in the skillet. Allow the eggs to set for a moment around the edges.

Add Herbs and Cheese:
- Sprinkle chopped fresh parsley, mint, and crumbled Feta cheese (if using) over the omelette.

Fold and Cook:
- Carefully fold the omelette in half or into thirds. Cook for an additional minute or until the eggs are fully cooked but still moist.

Serve:

- Slide the Shirazi Omelette onto a plate. Garnish with additional fresh herbs if desired.

Enjoy:
- Serve the Shirazi Omelette warm, either on its own or with a side of flatbread or toast.

This omelette captures the essence of Shirazi flavors with the inclusion of fresh herbs and vegetables. It's a versatile dish that can be customized based on personal preferences, and it makes for a delicious and wholesome breakfast or brunch option.

Kashk-o-Bademjan-e-Moraba

Ingredients:

- 2 medium-sized eggplants
- 1 cup kashk (fermented whey)
- 2 cloves garlic, minced
- 1 tablespoon dried mint
- 1/4 cup olive oil
- Salt and pepper to taste
- Fruit preserves or moraba (such as apricot or fig)
- Fresh herbs for garnish (parsley or mint)

Instructions:

Roast Eggplants:
- Preheat the oven to 400°F (200°C). Roast the eggplants in the oven until the skin is charred and the flesh is soft. Allow them to cool.

Prepare Eggplant Mash:
- Peel the roasted eggplants and mash the flesh in a bowl. Add minced garlic, dried mint, salt, and pepper. Mix well.

Add Kashk:
- Gradually add kashk to the mashed eggplants, mixing until you achieve a smooth and creamy consistency. Adjust seasoning to taste.

Drizzle with Olive Oil:
- Drizzle olive oil over the Kashk-o-Bademjan mixture for added richness.

Serve with Moraba:
- Spoon the Kashk-o-Bademjan onto a serving dish. Create a well in the center and add a dollop of your favorite fruit preserve or moraba.

Garnish:
- Garnish the dish with fresh herbs such as parsley or mint.

Serve:
- Serve the Kashk-o-Bademjan-e-Moraba with flatbread or as a dip. Enjoy the fusion of savory and slightly sweet flavors.

Keep in mind that this is a creative and hypothetical fusion dish. If you were referring to a specific traditional dish, please provide more details, and I'll be happy to help with a more accurate recipe.

Aloo Mosamma

Ingredients:

- 4 large potatoes, peeled and cut into cubes
- 2 tablespoons vegetable oil
- 1 large onion, finely chopped
- 2 cloves garlic, minced
- 2 large tomatoes, diced
- 2 tablespoons tomato paste
- 2 tablespoons pomegranate molasses (or sour grape juice)
- 1 teaspoon ground turmeric
- 1 teaspoon ground cumin
- Salt and pepper to taste
- Fresh herbs for garnish (parsley or cilantro)
- Optional: Saffron threads soaked in warm water for added flavor and color

Instructions:

Prepare Potatoes:
- Peel and cut the potatoes into cubes.

Sauté Onions and Garlic:
- In a pot, heat vegetable oil over medium heat. Sauté finely chopped onions until they become golden brown. Add minced garlic and cook for an additional minute.

Add Spices:
- Stir in ground turmeric and ground cumin. Mix well to coat the onions and garlic.

Add Tomatoes and Tomato Paste:
- Add diced tomatoes and tomato paste to the pot. Cook until the tomatoes are softened and the mixture is well combined.

Add Potatoes:
- Add the cubed potatoes to the pot. Mix them with the tomato-onion mixture.

Pour Souring Agent:
- Pour pomegranate molasses (or sour grape juice) over the potatoes. If using saffron, add the soaked saffron threads along with the water.

Season:
- Season the stew with salt and pepper according to your taste. Stir well to ensure even seasoning.

Simmer:
- Cover the pot and let the stew simmer on low heat until the potatoes are fully cooked and the flavors have melded together. Stir occasionally.

Garnish:
- Once the potatoes are tender, garnish the Aloo Mosamma with fresh herbs such as parsley or cilantro.

Serve:
- Serve the Aloo Mosamma hot, either on its own or with rice or bread.

Aloo Mosamma is known for its delightful combination of sour and savory flavors. The pomegranate molasses or sour grape juice adds a unique tanginess to the dish. Adjust the souring agent and seasoning according to your preference.

Dolmeh Barg

Ingredients:

- 1 pound (about 500g) beef or lamb sirloin, thinly sliced
- 1 large onion, grated
- 2 cloves garlic, minced
- 2 tablespoons plain yogurt
- 2 tablespoons olive oil
- Juice of 1 lemon
- 1 teaspoon ground saffron, dissolved in a bit of warm water
- Salt and pepper to taste
- Metal or bamboo skewers, soaked in water if using bamboo

Instructions:

Marinate the Meat:
- In a bowl, combine grated onion, minced garlic, plain yogurt, olive oil, lemon juice, ground saffron, salt, and pepper. Mix well to create the marinade.

Prepare the Meat:
- Slice the beef or lamb sirloin into thin, long strips. Add the sliced meat to the marinade, ensuring that each piece is well coated. Let it marinate for at least 2 hours or preferably overnight in the refrigerator.

Skewer the Meat:
- Thread the marinated meat onto skewers. If using bamboo skewers, make sure they have been soaked in water to prevent burning.

Grill the Kebabs:
- Preheat a grill or grill pan to medium-high heat. Grill the skewers for about 6-8 minutes, turning occasionally, until the meat is cooked and has a nice char.

Serve:
- Once the Dolmeh Barg is grilled to perfection, serve it hot with rice or flatbread. Optionally, garnish with additional saffron-infused water for extra flavor and a vibrant color.

Dolmeh Barg is a delicious and flavorful kebab that showcases the essence of Persian grilling. The marinade infuses the meat with a blend of aromatic spices, creating a succulent and savory dish.

Mirza Ghasemi Stuffed Mushrooms

Ingredients:

- Button mushrooms, cleaned and stems removed
- 1 cup Mirza Ghasemi mixture (smoked eggplant, tomatoes, garlic) - You can make Mirza Ghasemi separately and then use it for stuffing.
- 1/2 cup Feta cheese, crumbled
- Fresh parsley, chopped (for garnish)
- Olive oil
- Salt and pepper to taste

Instructions:

Prepare Mirza Ghasemi Mixture:
- Make a batch of Mirza Ghasemi by smoking eggplant, sautéing with tomatoes, garlic, and spices until it forms a thick mixture. Allow it to cool.

Prepare Mushrooms:
- Preheat the oven to 375°F (190°C).
- Clean the mushrooms and remove the stems. Place the mushroom caps on a baking sheet.

Stuff the Mushrooms:
- Spoon a generous amount of Mirza Ghasemi mixture into each mushroom cap, filling the cavity.

Add Feta Cheese:
- Sprinkle crumbled Feta cheese on top of the Mirza Ghasemi mixture in each mushroom.

Drizzle with Olive Oil:
- Drizzle a little olive oil over each stuffed mushroom for added flavor.

Season:
- Season the stuffed mushrooms with salt and pepper to taste.

Bake:
- Bake in the preheated oven for about 15-20 minutes or until the mushrooms are tender and the filling is heated through.

Garnish:
- Remove the stuffed mushrooms from the oven and sprinkle chopped fresh parsley on top for garnish.

Serve:
- Arrange the Mirza Ghasemi Stuffed Mushrooms on a serving platter and serve warm.

These Mirza Ghasemi Stuffed Mushrooms combine the smoky flavors of Mirza Ghasemi with the earthiness of mushrooms, creating a delicious and unique appetizer. Enjoy!

Mast-o-Khiar Stuffed Grape Leaves

Ingredients:

- Grape leaves, preserved or fresh, blanched
- 1 cup Mast-o-Khiar mixture (yogurt with cucumber, mint, and garlic)
- 1/2 cup cooked rice
- 1/4 cup ground walnuts
- 2 tablespoons raisins, finely chopped
- 1 tablespoon lemon juice
- Salt and pepper to taste
- Olive oil for drizzling
- Fresh mint leaves for garnish

Instructions:

Prepare Grape Leaves:
- If using preserved grape leaves, rinse them well to remove excess brine. If using fresh grape leaves, blanch them in boiling water for a few minutes until they are soft and pliable. Drain and set aside.

Prepare Mast-o-Khiar Mixture:
- In a bowl, combine Mast-o-Khiar (yogurt with cucumber, mint, and garlic).

Prepare Filling:
- Add cooked rice, ground walnuts, chopped raisins, lemon juice, salt, and pepper to the Mast-o-Khiar mixture. Mix well to create the filling.

Stuff Grape Leaves:
- Lay out a grape leaf, place a spoonful of the Mast-o-Khiar mixture in the center, and add a small amount of the filling.
- Fold the sides of the grape leaf over the filling and roll it up, creating a small stuffed roll. Repeat the process for the remaining grape leaves and filling.

Arrange in a Dish:
- Arrange the stuffed grape leaves in a serving dish, placing them snugly next to each other.

Drizzle with Olive Oil:
- Drizzle olive oil over the stuffed grape leaves for added richness.

Chill:
- Refrigerate the Mast-o-Khiar Stuffed Grape Leaves for at least 1-2 hours to allow the flavors to meld and the dish to chill.

Garnish:
- Before serving, garnish with fresh mint leaves.

Serve:
- Serve the Mast-o-Khiar Stuffed Grape Leaves chilled as a refreshing appetizer.

These stuffed grape leaves offer a delightful combination of creamy Mast-o-Khiar, nutty walnuts, and sweet raisins, all wrapped in tender grape leaves. Enjoy this unique and flavorful Persian appetizer!

www.ingramcontent.com/pod-product-compliance
Lightning Source LLC
LaVergne TN
LVHW081613060526
838201LV00054B/2224